GOOD
without gluten

FRÉDÉRIQUE JULES,
JENNIFER LEPOUTRE & MITSURU YANASE

PHOTOGRAPHS BY AKIKO IDA
STYLING BY SABRINA FAUDA-RÔLE

MURDOCH BOOKS

Table of contents

▼▼▼▼▼

Intro

▼▼▼▼▼

GOOD without GLUTEN is not a book about a passing trend, it's about a different way of cooking for people with coeliac disease or gluten intolerance, or anyone who wants to change their diet. It's a different approach to cooking and food because we work around dietary restrictions while at the same time exploring new culinary pleasures.

NOGLU, my restaurant in Paris, is the realisation of a dream of mine after ten years of culinary discoveries and disappointments. Years of research have gone into creating these recipes as I've tried to work out how to best combine a gluten intolerance with a growing interest in cooking and good food. Years of travelling, meeting people and experimenting with recipes inspired me to open a restaurant where people affected by similar dietary restrictions can enjoy simple, tasty, beautiful dishes that are good without gluten! Thanks to my fellow chefs Jenni, Mitsuru and Mike for their imagination and their total commitment to making NOGLU a place of culinary conviviality for everyone.

FRÉDÉRIQUE

The gluten-free pantry

▼ ▼ ▼ ▼ ▼

There are many gluten-free grains and flours and they offer a multitude of combinations for delicious baking and cooking. Their flavours and textures are often new and surprising, and the research we carried out when developing the dishes for our restaurant means we can offer you recipes that are attractive on both a nutritional level and in terms of flavour. All the products we use are certified gluten-free.

On the next few pages you'll find lists of the different ingredients you can gather together at home for easy and tasty gluten-free cooking every day. We also incorporate dairy substitutes in our recipes, because lactose intolerance often goes hand in hand with gluten intolerance, and these dairy substitutes offer their own nutritional value and flavour variations as well. You can find all these ingredients in organic food stores or on specialist websites.

Flours

▼▼▼▼▼

CHESTNUT FLOUR

We use chestnut flour in small quantities in combination with rice flour or tapioca and potato starch. It has a very strong flavour that gives lots of character to breads and baked items. It is also a food that's high in energy and low in fat.

MILLET FLOUR

Millet is an energy-rich, nutritious grain that's high in protein. Its flour has a neutral flavour and it gives body and softness to gluten-free baking.

BROWN RICE FLOUR

Rice flour is light and has a neutral flavour, so it is perfect to use as a base in baking in combination with other more strongly flavoured flours. It is high in nutrients and easy to digest.

CHICKPEA FLOUR (BESAN)

Energy-rich and high in protein, fibre and vitamins, this flour is used as the base for our bread, giving it a solid and soft structure. Yellow in colour and very mildly flavoured, it combines perfectly with chestnut or buckwheat flour to give variety of flavour and colour to gluten-free bread.

BUCKWHEAT FLOUR

With a strong, nutty flavour, this flour pairs very well with rice flour both in bread and baking. It provides body and softness. It is a highly nutritious grain, with plenty of fibre and antioxidants.

CORN FLOUR (MAIZE FLOUR)

Corn flour contains starch, protein and a small amount of fat from the germ. A fine flour can be made from the kernels and it is an excellent gluten-free flour for baking in combination with rice or millet flour.

Grains

▼▼▼▼▼

BLACK RICE

Highly nutritious, this rice — with a flavour that's reminiscent of hazelnuts — is rich in iron and fibre. Its dark purple colour is mainly due to its high mineral content. Like most rices, it contains several important amino acids.

SHORT-GRAIN BROWN RICE

Made up of the whole grain that still has its brownish outer layer of rice bran and germ, brown rice is easier to digest and more nutritious than white rice because the bran is high in fibre, vitamins and minerals.

QUINOA

A herbaceous plant that's grown for its protein-rich seeds, quinoa is considered to be a 'pseudocereal' because it is not part of the true grass family but one that also includes rhubarb and spinach. It is highly digestible and low in fat but high in iron, amino acids and proteins. It has a slightly nutty flavour.

LENTILS

Part of the legume family, lentils are high in minerals, protein and fibre, and are an excellent complement to vegetables.

RICE NOODLES

These are made from rice flour. Their cooking should be brief and controlled because they can become very sticky.

PASTA

The gluten-free macaroni we use is made from a combination of corn flour (maize flour) and rice flour, which means the pasta holds together better when cooked. Nevertheless, it should be closely watched when cooking as it breaks apart easily.

POLENTA

Polenta is a form of cornmeal. It gives thickness and a grainy texture to baked items and some savoury preparations.

Groceries

▼▼▼▼▼

POTATO STARCH

A starch extracted from potato tubers, it helps bind flours together and so alleviates the 'friable' tendency of gluten-free baked items.

TAPIOCA STARCH

Produced from dried cassava, it helps bind and lighten a mix of gluten-free flours.

ALMOND MEAL

Almonds add protein and fat, and therefore binding agents, to gluten-free baking.

GUAR GUM

A plant fibre in powder form, guar gum thickens and stabilises gluten-free preparations.

XANTHAN GUM

A food additive that comes in the form of an odourless white powder, xanthan has strong thickening and 'gluing' powers, an essential resource in gluten-free cooking, which can too often be crumbly.

WHOLE CANE SUGAR

Preferable to white sugar, which is devoid of any nutritional value, cane sugar still contains its natural vitamins and minerals.

PLANT MILKS

Rice, almond and soy milk are high in antioxidants, minerals and vitamins. These milks are an ideal alternative, in place of cow's milk, for all lactose-free preparations.

OILS

Olive oil, canola oil or lactose-free vegetable margarine are ideal for gluten-free cooking. We also use coconut oil in our baking, which adds its own little extra flavour.

Base n°1

Bread dough

▼ ▼ ▼ ▼ ▼

Makes a 1 kg (2 lb 4 oz) loaf
Preparation time: 15 minutes

3 eggs
1½ tablespoons
   olive oil
1 teaspoon cider
   vinegar
435 ml (15¼ fl oz/
   1¾ cups) water
2 tablespoons chickpea
   flour (besan)
125 g (4½ oz/¾ cup)
   rice flour

125 g (4½ oz/1 cup)
   tapioca starch
125 g (4½ oz)
   potato starch
2 teaspoons salt
1 tablespoon sugar
3 teaspoons
   xanthan gum
1 tablespoon
   dried yeast

Beat the eggs, olive oil, vinegar and water together in a mixer.

Combine the flours, starches, salt, sugar and xanthan gum in a bowl, then add the yeast. Pour these dry ingredients into the bowl of the mixer and beat for 2 minutes on a low speed. This dough is a base that you can add interest to with seeds, dried fruit, nuts, etc. (see Breads chapter).

Flour mix

FOR CAKES AND PASTRIES

▼ ▼ ▼ ▼ ▼

Makes 680 g (1 lb 8 oz)
Preparation time: 5 minutes

320 g (11¼ oz/2 cups) rice flour
240 g (8½ oz/2 cups) cornflour (cornstarch)
100 g (3½ oz/1 cup) almond meal
2 teaspoons xanthan gum

Place all the ingredients in a large bowl and mix well with a whisk. Store in an airtight container. This mixture of dry ingredients will be used as a base for the biscuit and cake recipes in this book, which you can use as starting points for multiple variations by adding or replacing ingredients: eggs, sugar, oil, milk, chocolate, etc. Don't hesitate to make up a large quantity of flour mix in advance and store it in an airtight container for later use.

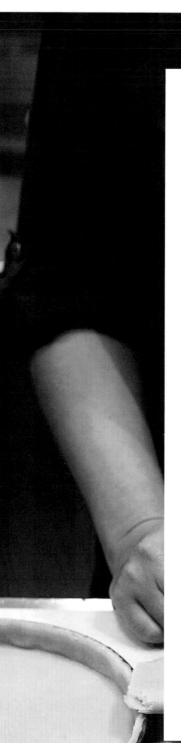

Sweet pastry

▼ ▼ ▼ ▼ ▼

Makes 1 large tart
Preparation time: 10 minutes
Resting time: overnight
Cooking time: 16 minutes

80 g (2¾ oz/½ cup)
  brown rice flour
45 g (1½ oz) cornflour
  (cornstarch)
40 g (1½ oz)
  almond meal
50 g (1¾ oz/⅓ cup) icing
  (confectioners') sugar

¼ teaspoon
  xanthan gum
80 g (2¾ oz) cold butter,
  cut into cubes
1 egg

Combine the rice flour, cornflour, almond meal, icing sugar and xanthan gum in the bowl of a mixer. Start mixing gently with the flat beater of the mixer (the non-cutting attachment). Little by little add the cubes of cold butter, mixing on a low speed until the mixture resembles breadcrumbs. Add the egg and keep mixing slowly until a ball of dough forms. Remove from the mixer and wrap with plastic wrap. Place in the refrigerator for several hours or overnight. The next day, roll out the dough to the desired size, lay it in the dish you are using and prick with a fork at regular intervals.

Tip: If you blind bake the dough, use baking paper over the base and scatter dried beans or ovenproof weights on top to prevent it from rising.

Base n°4

Savoury pastry

▼ ▼ ▼ ▼ ▼

Makes 1 large tart
Preparation time: 10 minutes
Cooking time: 15 minutes

140 g (5 oz) rice flour
30 g (1 oz/¼ cup)
  millet flour
30 g (1 oz/¼ cup)
  tapioca starch
35 g (1¼ oz)
  potato starch
55 g (2 oz) almond meal

1 teaspoon
  xanthan gum
1 teaspoon salt
100 g (3½ oz) cold
  butter, cut into cubes
1 egg, lightly beaten
1 tablespoon cold water

Combine the flours, starches, almond meal, xanthan gum and salt in a bowl. Add the butter to the dry mixture. Work together by hand until you have a 'crumbly' mixture. Add the egg and water and knead until a ball of dough forms. If the dough is too dry or doesn't hold together, add a little more water. Roll out the dough and cut to the size of the pie or tart (flan) dish.

Tip: You may find it easier to roll the dough on a sheet of baking paper and then use this to help you line the tin. If the pastry cracks or breaks, just press it into the tin with your fingers.

GLUTEN-FREE

Breakfasts

CRANBERRY-ORANGE *scones*

Makes 8–10 scones

Preparation time: 15 minutes
Cooking time: 20 minutes

500 g (1 lb 2 oz) gluten-free flour mix
    (page 13), plus extra for rolling
2 generous tablespoons baking powder
100 g (3½ oz) sugar
1 teaspoon salt
Finely grated zest of 2 oranges
150 g (5½ oz) cold butter, cut into cubes
150 g (5½ oz) dried cranberries
3 eggs
310 ml (10¾ fl oz/1¼ cups) full-
    cream milk (or pouring cream)

Preheat oven to 180°C (350°F/Gas 4).

Combine the flour mix, baking powder, sugar, salt and orange zest in a bowl. Using your fingertips, work the butter into this mixture until it resembles breadcrumbs. Add the cranberries to the mixture.

In another bowl, combine two of the eggs with the milk and pour this mixture into the dry ingredients. Gently combine with a large spoon until you have a dough that holds together. Turn onto a floured surface.

Roll the dough out without overworking it, then cut out scones using a round cutter. Place on a baking tray. Brush the tops of the scones lightly with the beaten egg yolk from the remaining egg. Bake for 18–20 minutes. Watch the scones carefully as they cook; they should be nicely browned.

Serve warm with butter and jam.

banana CAKE

Serves 12

(1 large loaf or 12 muffins)
Preparation time: 15 minutes
Cooking time: 1 hour for loaf; 25 minutes
for muffins

6 bananas
160 g (5½ oz/1 cup) rice flour
140 g (5 oz) almond meal
100 g (3½ oz) ground hazelnuts
2 tablespoons cornflour (cornstarch)
1 teaspoon xanthan gum
1 teaspoon salt
2 teaspoons baking powder
4 eggs, separated
240 g (8½ oz/1 cup) vergeoise
    sugar (see note)
2 tablespoons canola oil, plus
    extra for greasing
Chocolate chips and crushed
    hazelnuts, to decorate

NOTE: Vergeoise sugar is a soft brown sugar made from beets. It has a rich caramel flavour and comes in light (blond) and dark (brune), and can be substituted with either light or dark muscavado sugar, or soft brown sugar.

Preheat oven to 180°C (350°F/Gas 4).

Mash the bananas. Combine all the dry ingredients in a bowl.

Beat the egg whites to soft peaks with the sugar. Add the oil and mashed bananas and combine. Add the dry ingredients and mix to make a smooth batter.

Grease a 2.5 litre (87 fl oz/10 cup) loaf (bar) tin or the holes of a 185 ml (6 fl oz/¾ cup) muffin tin. Pour in the batter and scatter over the chocolate chips and nuts. Bake for 1 hour (or 25 minutes for muffins) or until a skewer inserted into the middle comes out clean. Let it cool in the tin and turn out when cold.

Delicious with: A good green tea.

carrot CAKE

Serves 10–12

Preparation time: 25 minutes
Cooking time: 45 minutes
Resting time: 1 hour

240 g (8½ oz) sugar
2 eggs
100 ml (3½ fl oz) canola oil,
   plus extra for greasing
60 g (2¼ oz/¼ cup) soy yoghurt
200 g (7 oz) gluten-free
   flour mix (page 13)
½ teaspoon salt
1 teaspoon baking powder
1 teaspoon bicarbonate of
   soda (baking soda)
2½ teaspoons ground cinnamon
½ teaspoon ground cloves
170 g (6 oz) carrot, grated

Icing (frosting)
50 g (1¾ oz) butter (or vegetable
   margarine), softened
150 g (5½ oz) cream cheese,
   at room temperature
340 g (12 oz/2¾ cups) icing
   (confectioners') sugar, sifted
1 pinch ground cinnamon

Preheat oven to 180°C (350°F/Gas 4).

Whisk the sugar with the eggs in a bowl, then add the oil and yoghurt and mix to combine. Combine the dry ingredients in another bowl, then pour them into the egg mixture and mix together until smooth.

Add the grated carrot, stirring constantly.

Grease a 24 cm (9½ inch) round cake tin and pour the batter into the tin. Bake for about 45 minutes or until a skewer inserted into the middle comes out clean. Allow to cool.

Meanwhile, to make the icing, beat the butter in the bowl of a mixer on a low speed until smooth. Add the cream cheese in several batches and beat until smooth and creamy. Add the icing sugar and cinnamon and mix well. Refrigerate for about 1 hour until quite firm, then use a piping (icing) bag to decorate the carrot cake with the cream cheese icing.

pear-almond  MUFFINS

Makes 10 muffins

Preparation time: 15 minutes
Cooking time: 20 minutes

240 g (8½ oz) gluten-free
   flour mix (page 13)
30 g (1 oz) almond meal
2 teaspoons baking powder
1 large pear
1 vanilla bean, halved lengthways
   and seeds scraped
60 g (2¼ oz/¼ cup) vegetable margarine
2 eggs
250 ml (9 fl oz/1 cup) milk (soy or rice)
50 g (1¾ oz/½ cup) flaked almonds

Preheat oven to 180°C (350°F/Gas 4).

Combine all the dry ingredients together.

Peel the pear and poach in 300 ml (10½ fl oz) boiling water with the vanilla bean and seeds. Drain and cool the pear, then dice.

Melt the margarine and use a whisk or mixer to combine with the eggs and milk. Incorporate the dry ingredients into this mixture and stir to make a smooth batter. Add the poached pear.

Line ten 80 ml (2½ fl oz/⅓ cup) muffin holes with paper cases and divide the mixture between them. Sprinkle a few flaked almonds on top and bake for 20 minutes, checking the muffins towards the end of the cooking time.

pancakes

Serves 4

Makes about 10–12 pancakes
Preparation time: 10 minutes
Cooking time: 30 minutes

260 g (9¼ oz) gluten-free
    flour mix (page 13)
4 tablespoons sugar
½ teaspoon salt
2 teaspoons baking powder
1 teaspoon bicarbonate of
    soda (baking soda)
480 ml (16¼ fl oz) milk (or
    soy or rice milk)
2 eggs
80 g (2¾ oz) butter (or vegetable
    margarine), melted
Butter (or vegetable
    margarine), for frying

Mix together the flour mix, sugar, salt, baking powder
and bicarbonate of soda.

In another bowl, mix the milk and eggs together,
add the melted butter, then add this mixture to the dry
ingredients. Mix thoroughly with a wooden spatula to
make a smooth batter.

Heat a frying pan over medium heat and melt a knob
of butter. Pour in a ladleful of batter to make a pancake
about 8–10 cm (3¼–4 inches) across. Cook until bubbles
form on the surface of the batter, then flip the pancake
and cook until golden brown. Repeat with the remaining
mixture. Serve with syrup and fruit of your choice.

qranola MIX WITH GOJI BERRIES

Makes 1 kg (2 lb 4 oz) granola
Preparation time: 10 minutes
Cooking time: 25 minutes

200 g (7 oz) rice flakes
200 g (7 oz) buckwheat flakes
100 g (3½ oz) chestnut flakes
100 g (3½ oz) raisins
200 g (7 oz/1¼ cups) whole
   almonds, roughly chopped
100 g (3½ oz) whole hazelnuts,
   roughly chopped
200 ml (7 fl oz) orange juice
100 ml (3½ fl oz) olive oil
1 tablespoon vergeoise blonde or light
   brown sugar (see note page 22)
100 g (3½ oz) honey
100 g (3½ oz) goji berries

Preheat oven to 120°C (235°F/Gas ½).

Combine all the flakes with the raisins in a large bowl. Add the chopped nuts.

Make a syrup by combining the orange juice, olive oil and sugar. Pour this syrup over the flake mixture and mix well so that the granola is thoroughly coated with the syrup.

Line a baking tray with baking paper and spread out the granola on it. Lightly drizzle over the honey. Bake for 20–25 minutes, turning from time to time, until the granola has a good golden colour, but make sure the raisins don't burn.

Remove the granola from the oven, allow to cool and then pour into a large container. Add the goji berries while the mixture is still warm.

Serve with soy yoghurt, some seasonal fresh fruit and a little honey.

Storing: The granola keeps for a maximum of 15 days in an airtight storage jar.

BANANA–BLUEBERRY RICE MILK *smoothie*

Preparation time: 5 minutes

500 ml (17 fl oz/2 cups) rice
 milk, well chilled
2 bananas
1 teaspoon agave syrup
125 g (4½ oz) blueberries
1 tablespoon whole almond butter

Put all the ingredients into a blender. Blend for 2 minutes, pour into a tall glass and enjoy for an energising breakfast.

Variation: The rice milk can be replaced with almond milk.

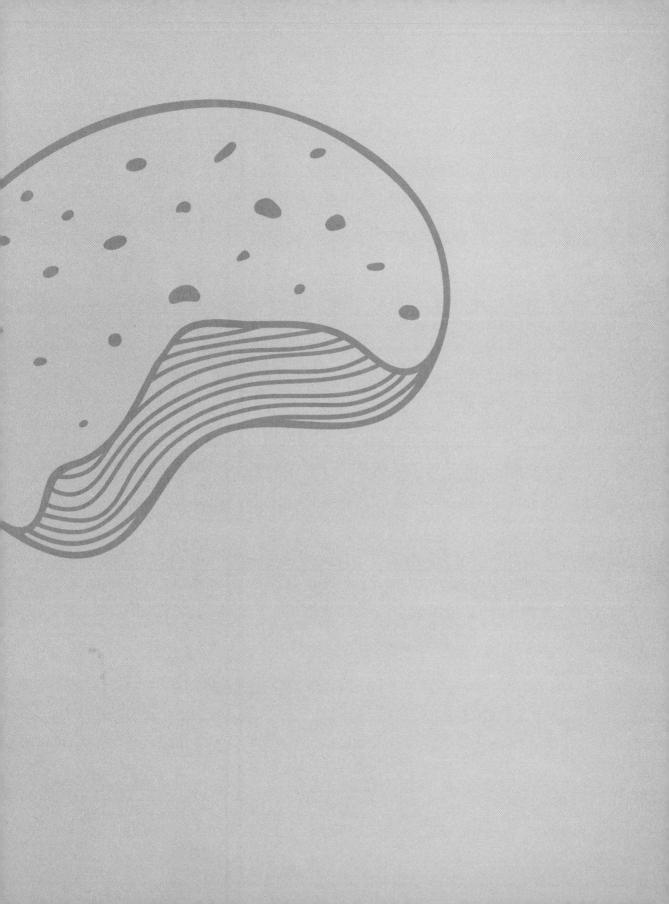

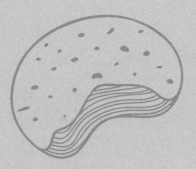

GLUTEN-FREE

Afternoon Tea

chocolate chip COOKIES

Makes about 20 cookies

Preparation time: 15 minutes
Resting time: 1 hour
Cooking time: 15 minutes

200 g (7 oz) butter
150 g (5½ oz) vergeoise blonde or light
   brown sugar (see note page 22)
165 g (5¾ oz/¾ cup) caster
   (superfine) sugar
2 eggs
290 g (10¼ oz) gluten-free
   flour mix (page 13)
1 teaspoon baking powder
1 teaspoon salt
250 g (9 oz) chocolate chips

Preheat oven to 180°C (350°F/Gas 4).

Beat the butter with both sugars in a mixer until well combined. Add the eggs, one at a time, mixing well after each.

In another bowl, combine all the dry ingredients with the chocolate chips. Add the dry ingredients to the mixer bowl and combine well using a large spoon.

Make balls from the dough (you can use a small ice-cream scoop) and place the balls on a baking tray lined with baking paper. Refrigerate for at least 1 hour until the dough is firm. (It's even better to let it rest overnight.)

Remove the tray from the refrigerator and place it straight into the oven. Bake for 6 minutes, then turn the tray around and bake for 6 minutes more. Remove from the oven and cool on the tray.

Storing: These cookies keep very well for 2–3 days in an airtight cake tin.

triple chocolate COOKIES

Makes about 20 cookies

Preparation time: 15 minutes
Resting time: 1 hour
Cooking time: 15 minutes

200 g (7 oz) butter
155 g (5½ oz) vergeoise blonde or light
  brown sugar (see note page 22)
155 g (5½ oz) caster (superfine) sugar
2 eggs
260 g (9¼ oz) rice flour
30 g (1 oz/¼ cup) cocoa powder
1 teaspoon baking powder
1 teaspoon salt
125 g (4½ oz) white chocolate,
  chopped (or chips)
125 g (4½ oz) dark chocolate,
  chopped (or chips)

Preheat oven to 180°C (350°F/Gas 4).

Beat the butter with the two sugars in a mixer until well combined. Add the eggs, one at a time, mixing well after each.

In another bowl, combine all the dry ingredients with the two kinds of chocolate.

Add the dry ingredients to the bowl of the mixer and mix well using a large spoon.

Make balls from the dough (you can use a small ice-cream scoop) and place the balls on a baking tray lined with baking paper. Place in the refrigerator for at least 1 hour until the dough is firm. (It's even better to let it rest overnight.)

Remove the tray from the refrigerator and place it straight into the oven. Bake for 6 minutes, then turn the tray around and bake for 6 minutes more. When you remove them from the oven, let them cool on the tray.

raisin-choc-coconut COOKIES

Makes about 20 cookies

Preparation time: 15 minutes
Resting time: 1 hour
Cooking time: 15 minutes

110 g (3¾ oz) butter
220 g (7¾ oz) vergeoise sugar
  (see note page 22)
1 egg
210 g (7½ oz) gluten-free
  flour mix (page 13)
½ teaspoon baking powder
½ teaspoon bicarbonate of
  soda (baking soda)
130 g (4½ oz/¾ cup) raisins
125 g (4½ oz/¾ cup) chocolate chips
125 g (4½ oz/1 cup) chopped walnuts
125 g (4½ oz) desiccated coconut

Preheat oven to 180°C (350°F/Gas 4).

Beat the butter with the sugar in a mixer until well combined. Add the egg and mix well.

In another bowl, combine all the dry ingredients with the raisins, chocolate chips, walnuts and coconut. Add these dry ingredients to the butter mix and combine well using a large spoon.

Make balls from the dough (you can use a small ice-cream scoop) and place the balls on a baking tray lined with baking paper. Refrigerate for at least 1 hour until the dough is firm. (It's even better to let it rest overnight.)

Remove the tray from the refrigerator and place it straight into the oven. Bake for 6 minutes, then turn the tray around and bake for 6 minutes more. Once removed from the oven, let them cool on the tray.

shortbread BISCUITS

Makes about 30 biscuits
Preparation time: 10 minutes
Cooking time: 15 minutes

100 g (3½ oz/¾ cup) corn
   flour (maize flour)
100 g (3½ oz) rice flour, plus
   extra for dusting
100 g (3½ oz/¾ cup) coconut flour
   (from organic food stores)
100 g (3½ oz/1 cup) almond meal
100 g (3½ oz) icing (confectioners') sugar
½ teaspoon salt
250 g (9 oz) cold butter, cut into cubes
1 egg yolk

Preheat oven to 170°C (325°F/Gas 3).
   Combine the flours, almond meal, icing sugar and salt. Add the butter and rub with your fingers until the mixture resembles breadcrumbs.
   Add the egg yolk and knead again with your hands until you have a smooth dough. Form into a ball. Dust a clean surface with rice flour and roll out the dough until 5 mm (¼ inch) thick. Use a cookie cutter to cut out biscuits in whatever shape you prefer. Place them on a baking tray lined with baking paper. Bake for about 15 minutes or until golden.

lemon  CAKE

Serves 8

Preparation time: 15 minutes
Cooking time: 40 minutes

190 g (6¾ oz) gluten-free
    flour mix (page 13)
1 teaspoon bicarbonate of
    soda (baking soda)
150 g (5½ oz) sugar
2 eggs
80 ml (2½ fl oz) canola oil
200 ml (7 fl oz) soy milk (or rice
    milk), plus extra for brushing
Finely grated zest and juice of 1 lemon
Finely grated zest and juice of 1 lime

Syrup
Finely grated zest and juice of 1 lemon
60 g (2¼ oz/½ cup) icing
    (confectioners') sugar

Preheat oven to 200°C (400°F/Gas 6).

Combine the dry ingredients in a mixer bowl.

In another bowl, combine the eggs, canola oil and milk.

Add the wet ingredients to the dry ingredients and mix
to a smooth batter. Add the juice and zest of the lemon
and lime and stir through to combine.

Spoon the batter into a loaf (bar) tin, not filling more
than three-quarters full. Brush with about 1 tablespoon of
milk, then bake for 40 minutes or until a skewer inserted
into the middle comes out clean.

Make the syrup by heating the juice and zest of the
lemon with the icing sugar in a saucepan until they form
a syrup. Pour this over the warm cake.

CHESTNUT

Makes 10–12 crêpes
Preparation time: 5 minutes
Resting time: 2 hours
Cooking time: 30 minutes

2 eggs
375 ml (13 fl oz/1½ cups)
   milk (or plant milk)
1 tablespoon melted butter (or
   vegetable margarine)
130 g (4½ oz) gluten-free flour mix
   (page 13)
40 g (1½ oz) chestnut flour
1 pinch salt

Combine the eggs and milk in a bowl, then add the melted butter and mix to combine.

In another bowl, combine the flour mix, chestnut flour and the salt.

Add the wet ingredients to the dry ingredients, whisking well to remove any lumps. Refrigerate for 2 hours.

Stir the batter well before cooking the crêpes.

Melt a small teaspoon of butter in a hot frying pan. Pour a ladleful of batter into the frying pan and spread out to make a very thin layer. Brown on one side for about 2 minutes or until bubbles form on the surface, then flip with a spatula. Cook for another 2 minutes.

Enjoy with your favourite jam or a gluten-free chocolate spread.

Tip: It's best to make the batter the night before and let it rest in the refrigerator overnight.

RASPBERRY–PISTACHIO *friands*

Makes 12 friands

Preparation time: 15 minutes
Resting time: 1 hour
Cooking time: 15 minutes

130 g (4½ oz) butter, plus
   extra for greasing
50 g (1¾ oz) pistachios, ground
50 g (1¾ oz/½ cup) almond meal
90 g (3¼ oz) gluten-free
   flour mix (page 13)
175 g (6 oz) icing (confectioners') sugar
2 egg whites
250 g (9 oz/2 cups) fresh raspberries

Preheat oven to 180°C (350°F/Gas 4).

Heat the butter in a saucepan over medium heat until it turns a light brown colour and a few brown flecks appear. Stop the cooking process by dipping the base of the saucepan in cold water, then allow to cool.

Combine the ground pistachios, almond meal, flour mix and icing sugar.

Beat the egg whites by hand until they look foamy, then fold in to the dry ingredients. Pour this mixture into the cooled butter, mix well then allow to stand for 1 hour in the refrigerator.

Grease 12 friand moulds and fill them three-quarters full with the batter just taken out of the refrigerator. Divide the raspberries between the friands.

Bake for 15 minutes or until they spring back when gently pressed. Cool well before removing from the tin.

Delicious with: A Japanese green tea.

chocolate-coconut ROUGHS

Makes about 16

Preparation time: 10 minutes
Cooking time: 15 minutes

70 g (2½ oz) cocoa powder
360 g (12¾ oz) icing (confectioners') sugar
300 g (10½ oz/3⅓ cups) desiccated coconut
1 pinch salt
4 drops natural vanilla extract
4 egg whites

Preheat oven to 160°C (315°F/Gas 2–3).

Place all the dry ingredients and the vanilla extract into the bowl of a mixer fitted with a flat beater (the non-cutting attachment). Mix well. With the mixer still running, add the egg whites, one at a time, mixing well after each.

Line a baking tray with baking paper. Make balls from the dough (you can use a small ice-cream scoop) and place them on the baking paper. Space them 4 cm (1½ inches) apart.

Bake for 15 minutes.

lemon MUFFINS

Makes about 10 muffins

Preparation time: 15 minutes
Cooking time: 20 minutes

185 g (6½ oz) gluten-free
   flour mix (page 13)
1 teaspoon bicarbonate of
   soda (baking soda)
150 g (5½ oz) sugar
2 eggs
80 ml (2½ fl oz/⅓ cup) canola oil
200 ml (7 fl oz) soy milk (or rice milk)
Finely grated zest and juice of 1 lemon

Icing (frosting)
Finely grated zest and juice of 1 lime
25 g (1 oz) icing (confectioners') sugar

Preheat oven to 200°C (400°F/Gas 6).

Combine the dry ingredients in a mixer bowl.

In another bowl, combine the eggs, canola oil and milk. Add the lemon juice and zest, then pour into the dry ingredients. Mix until you have a smooth batter.

Line ten 80 ml (2½ fl oz/⅓ cup) muffin holes with paper cases and divide the mixture between them, filling each one only three-quarters full. Bake for about 20 minutes or until the muffins springs back when gently pressed.

Make the icing by heating the lime juice and zest with the icing sugar in a saucepan over medium heat until they form a pale thick syrup.

Pour a generous tablespoon of icing over each muffin and garnish with a raspberry or strawberry for a fruity and colourful finish.

chocolate MUFFINS

Makes 10 muffins

Preparation time: 15 minutes
Cooking time: 20 minutes

150 g (5½ oz) gluten-free
   flour mix (page 13)
30 g (1 oz/¼ cup) cocoa powder
1 teaspoon bicarbonate of
   soda (baking soda)
150 g (5½ oz) sugar
2 eggs
80 ml (2½ fl oz/⅓ cup) canola oil
200 ml (7 fl oz) soy milk (or rice milk)
50 g (1¾ oz) chocolate chips

Preheat oven to 200°C (400°F/Gas 6).

Combine the dry ingredients in a mixer bowl.

In another bowl, combine the eggs, canola oil and milk, then pour into the dry mixture. Mix until you have a smooth batter.

Line ten 80 ml (2½ fl oz/⅓ cup) muffin holes with paper cases and divide the mixture between them, filling each one only three-quarters full.

Sprinkle with the chocolate chips, then place in the oven and bake for 20 minutes or until the muffins spring back when pressed.

madeleines

Makes 12 large madeleines
Preparation time: 15 minutes
Resting time: 1 hour
Cooking time: 10–15 minutes

100 g (3½ oz) vegetable margarine,
   plus extra for greasing
2 eggs
80 g (2¾ oz) caster (superfine) sugar
70 g (2½ oz) gluten-free
   flour mix (page 13)
50 g (1¾ oz/½ cup) almond meal
1½ teaspoons baking powder
Zest of ½ a lemon

Preheat oven to 210°C (415°F/Gas 6–7).

Melt the margarine in a small saucepan over low heat.

Whisk the eggs and sugar together until light and creamy. Add the margarine gradually, mixing to keep the mixture smooth, then add all the dry ingredients and lemon zest.

Let the batter rest for at least 1 hour in the refrigerator.

Grease the madeleine moulds and fill with the batter to three-quarters full, using a piping (icing) bag to make it easier.

Cook for 5 minutes or until the 'hump' appears in the middle of each madeleine, then lower the oven temperature to 200°C (400°F/Gas 6) and cook for another 5–7 minutes or until the madeleines are golden. Let them cool for a few minutes before unmoulding.

chouquettes

Preparation time: 15 minutes
Cooking time: 20–25 minutes

90 g (3¼ oz) rice flour
35 g (1¼ oz) cornflour (cornstarch)
1 teaspoon xanthan gum
250 ml (9 fl oz/1 cup) water
110 g (3¾ oz) butter
1 pinch salt
5 eggs
1 egg yolk, lightly beaten
30 g (1 oz) pearl sugar

Preheat oven to 200°C (400°F/Gas 6).

Combine the rice flour, cornflour and xanthan gum in a bowl.

Put the water, butter and salt in a saucepan over medium heat. Once the butter has completely melted, bring the mixture to the boil, then remove from the heat. Pour the dry mixture into the saucepan and return to the heat. Mix until a ball of dough forms, then remove from the heat and continue to stir for a further 2 minutes to cool slightly.

Now add the eggs, one at a time. Each egg must be well incorporated into the dough before adding the next: the dough should be quite glossy and firm. You may not need the fifth egg.

Put the dough into a piping (icing) bag and pipe small balls onto a baking tray lined with baking paper. Use a pastry brush to brush each ball of dough with some beaten egg yolk. Sprinkle with pearl sugar.

Bake for 20–25 minutes or until the balls are well puffed up, golden and dry to the touch.

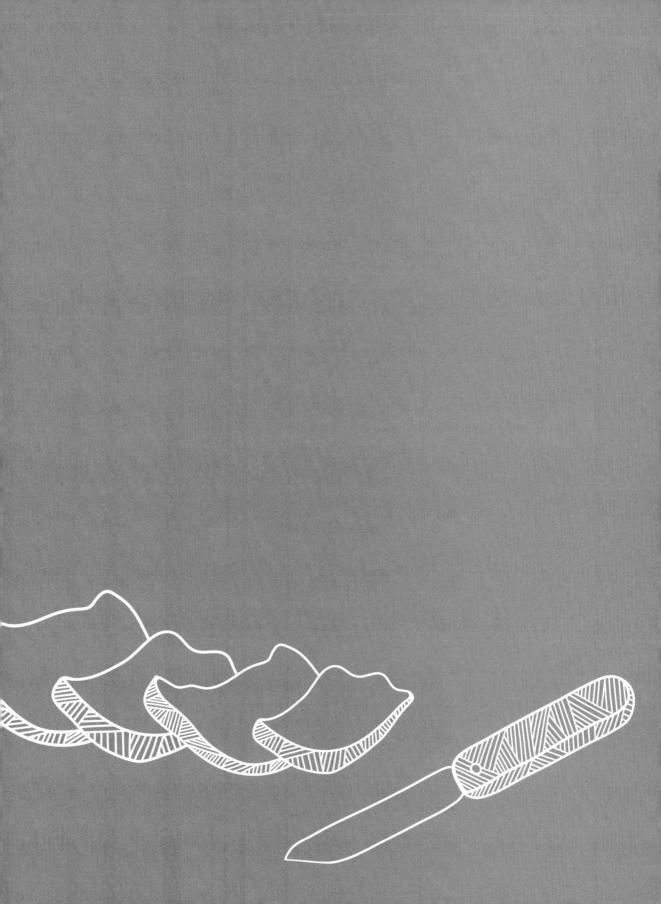

GLUTEN-FREE

Nibbles

grissini WITH HERBS

Makes 20 grissini

Preparation time: 15 minutes
Cooking time: 10–12 minutes

3 rosemary sprigs, leaves only
2 thyme sprigs, leaves only
1 quantity gluten-free bread
    dough (page 12)
Coarse salt and coarsely
    ground black pepper

Preheat oven to 180°C (350°F/Gas 4).

Roughly chop the rosemary and thyme leaves.

Place the bread dough in a piping (icing) bag with a 1 cm (½ inch) nozzle. Line a baking tray with baking paper. Pipe 20 lines of dough, each about 10–12 cm (4–4½ inches) long, onto the tray.

Sprinkle with coarse salt, pepper, rosemary and thyme.

Bake for 10 minutes. Turn the grissini and brown for a further 1–2 minutes so they are completely dry. Serve with cheese.

Variation: For cheese grissini, add 150 g (5½ oz) grated parmesan cheese to the dough before piping.

goat's cheese  AND GREEN OLIVE MUFFINS

Makes 12 muffins

Preparation time: 10 minutes
Cooking time: 15 minutes

200 g (7 oz) gluten-free
   flour mix (page 13)
2 teaspoons baking powder
3 eggs
2½ tablespoons olive oil
110 ml (3¾ fl oz) rice milk
100 g (3½ oz) goat's cheese, crumbled
100 g (3½ oz) pitted green olives
Salt and pepper

Preheat oven to 180°C (350°F/Gas 4).

Combine the flour mix and baking powder in a bowl.

Beat the eggs with the olive oil and rice milk, then add the goat's cheese, mixing well. Add the dry ingredients to the wet mixture and mix to produce a smooth batter. Add the olives and stir to combine. Season with salt and pepper.

Line twelve 80 ml (2½ fl oz/⅓ cup) muffin holes with paper cases and divide the mixture between them. Bake for 12–15 minutes or until the muffins are golden brown but remain springy to the touch.

pesto AND SUN-DRIED TOMATO MUFFINS

Makes 12 muffins

Preparation time: 10 minutes
Cooking time: 15 minutes

200 g (7 oz) gluten-free
  flour mix (page 13)
2 teaspoons baking powder
3 eggs
2½ tablespoons olive oil
110 ml (3¾ fl oz) rice milk
60 g (2¼ oz/¼ cup) pesto
100 g (3½ oz) sun-dried tomatoes,
  cut into small pieces
Salt and pepper

Preheat oven to 180°C (350°F/Gas 4).

Combine the flour mix and baking powder in a bowl.

Beat the eggs with the olive oil and rice milk, then add the pesto, mixing well with a whisk. Add the dry ingredients to the wet mixture and mix to produce a smooth batter. Add the sun-dried tomatoes. Adjust the seasoning with salt and pepper if necessary.

Line twelve 80 ml (2½ fl oz/⅓ cup) muffin holes with paper cases and divide the mixture between them. Bake for 12–15 minutes or until the muffins are golden brown but still springy to the touch.

focaccia  WITH FRESH HERBS

Serves 8

Preparation time: 5 minutes
Resting time: 30 minutes
Cooking time: 15–20 minutes

1 kg (2 lb 4 oz) gluten-free bread
    dough (page 12; you will need to
    make 1½ quantities of base recipe)
80 ml (2½ fl oz/⅓ cup) olive oil,
    plus extra for brushing
Coarse salt and coarsely
    ground black pepper
4 thyme sprigs, leaves only
4 rosemary sprigs, leaves only

Preheat oven to 180°C (350°F/Gas 4).

Brush a rectangular 20 × 28 cm (8 × 11¼ inch) baking tray with olive oil. Tip the dough into the tin and stretch out to about 2–4 cm (¾–1½ inches) thick. Smooth the surface of the dough with wet hands and let it rise under a cloth at room temperature for 30 minutes.

Scatter the top of the dough with salt and pepper and sprinkle over the thyme and rosemary leaves. Pour a drizzle of olive oil over the surface of the dough.

Cook for 15–20 minutes. Serve fresh out of the oven.

Nibble with: A fresh fruit juice.

PARMESAN *gougères*

Makes about 30
Preparation time: 15 minutes
Cooking time: 20 minutes

250 ml (9 fl oz/1 cup) water
100 g (3½ oz) vegetable margarine
2 pinches salt
150 g (5½ oz) rice flour
200 g (7 oz) parmesan cheese, grated
4 eggs

Preheat oven to 180°C (350°F/Gas 4).

In a saucepan, boil the water with the margarine and salt. Once the margarine has completely melted, add the rice flour and mix vigorously with a whisk.

Add 150 g (5½ oz) of the grated parmesan and the eggs and whisk until the dough is smooth and glossy.

Put the dough into a piping (icing) bag and pipe about 30 small balls onto a baking tray lined with baking paper.

Sprinkle over the remaining parmesan. Bake for 20 minutes. Serve immediately.

corn tortilla chips WITH GUACAMOLE

Serves 6

Preparation time: 20 minutes
Resting time: 1 hour
Cooking time: 10 minutes

2 ripe avocados
1 tablespoon lemon juice
1 tablespoon olive oil
1 tomato, diced
1 preserved lemon, rind finely chopped

Dough
150 g (5½ oz/1 cup) corn flour (maize
    flour), plus extra for dusting
40 g (1½ oz) vegetable margarine
2½ tablespoons water
½ teaspoon salt
3 tablespoons peanut oil, for frying

To make the dough, combine the flour, margarine, water and salt by hand to form a ball. Wrap the dough in plastic wrap and rest for 1 hour in the refrigerator.

To make the guacamole, peel the avocados, remove the stones and place the flesh in a food processor with the lemon juice and olive oil. Process until smooth. Tip into a bowl. Add the diced tomatoes and preserved lemon and season with salt and pepper. Keep the guacamole in the refrigerator.

Remove the ball of dough from the refrigerator, dust a clean surface with corn flour and roll out the dough until it is very thin. Cut into triangles. Heat the peanut oil in a large heavy-based frying pan and fry the triangles over medium heat until crisp and golden. Remove them with a slotted spoon. Salt lightly and serve immediately with the guacamole.

GLUTEN-FREE
Starters

MARINATED *salmon* WITH CITRUS AND QUINOA

Serves 4

Preparation time: 15 minutes
Resting time: 24 hours

2 French shallots, finely chopped
2 tablespoons olive oil
100 g (3½ oz/½ cup) quinoa
250 ml (9 fl oz/1 cup) water
½ preserved lemon, rind finely chopped
1 tablespoon capers, rinsed,
    finely chopped
1 small handful coriander
    (cilantro) leaves, finely chopped,
    plus extra to garnish
12 tarragon leaves, finely chopped
Flesh of 1 lemon (seeds removed),
    finely chopped
200 g (7 oz) very fresh salmon fillet

Marinade
220 g (7¾ oz/1 cup) sugar
100 g (3½ oz) salt
Finely grated zest and juice of 2 oranges
Finely grated zest and juice of 1 lemon

Sweat the shallots in a saucepan with 1 tablespoon of the olive oil for 4–5 minutes. Add the quinoa and sauté until almost translucent. Add the water and as soon as it comes to the boil, cover the saucepan, take off the heat and set aside for 20 minutes.

Add the preserved lemon, capers, coriander, tarragon and lemon flesh to the remaining olive oil and mix with the quinoa. Season to taste.

Combine the marinade ingredients. Place the salmon in a bowl. Add the marinade and turn the salmon to coat well. Cover and refrigerate for 24 hours. Rinse the salmon under cold water, dry and slice it into long, thin slices. Serve with the quinoa, a sprinkle of chopped coriander and some soy sauce.

Delicious with: Gluten-free blinis (see pancake recipe on page 28, and use the same ingredients, minus the sugar).

NoGlu SALAD

Serves 4

Preparation time: 10 minutes

100 g (3½ oz) mesclun
50 g (1¾ oz) rocket (arugula)
50 g (1¾ oz) mustard greens
100 g (3½ oz) beetroot (beets)
   of different colours
100 g (3½ oz) carrots
60 g (2¼ oz) blue cheese, crumbled
40 g (1½ oz/¼ cup) dried cranberries
30 g (1 oz) flaked almonds, toasted

Dressing
2 tablespoons olive oil
Juice of 1 lemon
1 teaspoon sweet gluten-free mustard

Wash the leaves and then dry in a salad spinner. Peel the beetroot and carrots and, using a mandoline, cut them into very thin slices.

Combine all of the dressing ingredients.

On shallow plates or wide bowls, arrange the salad leaves, then the sliced vegetables and cheese. Drizzle with the dressing and scatter over the cranberries and almonds.

Delicious with: A pizza or club sandwich.

pumpkin soup WITH CHESTNUTS

Serves 6–8

Preparation time: 15 minutes
Cooking time: 25 minutes

2–3 tablespoons olive oil
200 g (7 oz) French shallots, chopped
1 kg (2 lb 4 oz) pumpkin (winter squash),
 peeled and chopped into chunks
310 ml (10¾ fl oz/1¼ cups) chicken stock
 (or 1 organic stock/bouillon cube
 dissolved in 310 ml boiling water)
310 ml (10¾ fl oz/1¼ cups) water
500 ml (17 fl oz/2 cups) soy milk
50 g (1¾ oz) vegetable margarine
100 g (3½ oz) cooked and peeled
 chestnuts (sold in a jar or
 vacuum-packed), chopped
Chives and fresh herbs of choice,
 to garnish

Heat the olive oil in a saucepan. Add the shallots and cook for 4–5 minutes or until caramelised, then add the pumpkin and let it sweat for a few minutes. Add the chicken stock and water and simmer for 20 minutes or until the chunks of pumpkin are tender. Remove from the heat and add the soy milk, margarine and chestnuts.

Purée until smooth. Return to the heat to warm through.

Tip: Set aside a few caramelised shallots and a few pieces of chestnut for a garnish.

CORN *chiffon* CAKE

Serves 6–8

Preparation time: 20 minutes
Cooking time: 25 minutes

4 eggs, separated
65 ml (2 fl oz) soy milk
55 ml (1¾ fl oz) canola oil, plus
   extra for greasing
35 g (1¼ oz) rice flour
35 g (1¼ oz) cornflour (cornstarch)
60 g (2¼ oz) sugar

Preheat oven to 190°C (375°F/Gas 5).

Grease a chiffon, bundt or angel food cake tin — use a special tin with a central funnel or, if you don't have one, a loaf (bar) tin.

Combine 3 egg yolks (the fourth isn't used), soy milk and canola oil in a medium bowl. In a separate bowl, combine the flour and cornflour, then add to the egg mixture, stirring to combine. Whisk the 4 egg whites until soft peaks form, then add the sugar in three stages, whisking well until thick. Add a little of the egg white mixture to the egg yolk mixture and gently fold in, then carefully fold in the remaining egg white mixture in three stages.

Pour the batter into the cake tin. Bake for 25 minutes.

Cool for at least 1 hour in the tin, then unmould. Serve with some good lightly cooked (*mi-cuit*) foie gras.

SMOKED DUCK AND CARAMELISED LEEK *quiche*

Serves 6

Preparation time: 30 minutes
Resting time: 12 hours (for the pastry)
Cooking time: 35 minutes

1 quantity savoury pastry (page 16)
100 g (3½ oz) leek, pale part only,
    thinly sliced
40 g (1½ oz) vegetable margarine
20 g (¾ oz) duck fat (or vegetable
    margarine if preferred)
100 g (3½ oz) onion, sliced
120 g (4¼ oz) smoked duck breast,
    sliced
2 eggs
200 ml (7 fl oz) soy milk

Prepare the pastry and let it rest for a few hours, or overnight, before making the quiche.

Preheat oven to 180°C (350°F/Gas 4).

Line a 1 litre (35 fl oz/4 cup) tart (flan) tin or dish with the pastry and blind bake the tart base for 10–15 minutes or until golden brown (see tip on page 14).

Meanwhile, caramelise the leek in a frying pan with the margarine over medium heat.

Heat the duck fat in another frying pan, add the onion and cook over medium heat until caramelised. Place the leek on the pastry base, then top with the smoked duck and the caramelised onion.

Preheat the grill (broiler).

Beat the eggs and soy milk together with a whisk until well combined. Pour into the pastry base. Bake for 10 minutes, then place under the grill for 6–8 minutes or until the quiche is set and golden.

Serve with a raw vegetable salad.

summer ROLLS

Serves 6

Preparation time: 15 minutes
Cooking time: 10 minutes
Cooling time: 10 minutes

200 g (7 oz) raw king prawns
200 g (7 oz) raw crab claws
6 rice paper sheets
1 sucrine, little gem or baby cos
   (romaine) lettuce, sliced
200 g (7 oz) daikon (white radish),
   cut into matchsticks
6 spring onions (scallions)
6 mint sprigs, plus extra to garnish
1 bunch coriander (cilantro)
Salt

Sesame sauce
100 g (3½ oz/⅔ cup) sesame seeds
1 tablespoon white wine
2 teaspoons mirin (rice wine)
1½ tablespoons natural yoghurt

Cook the prawns and crab claws in boiling salted water. Remove from the hot water, plunge into cold water to stop them cooking further and allow to cool before removing their shells.

Moisten the rice paper sheets in a bowl of water, then drain and lay out flat on a tea towel (dish towel). Place one-sixth of the lettuce, daikon, crab and prawns on the rice paper, then top with a spring onion, a mint sprig and some coriander. Roll up tightly so the filling holds together and the roll takes shape. Cut into 4 pieces. Repeat with the remaining ingredients and garnish with a few extra mint leaves.

For the sauce, toast the sesame seeds in a dry frying pan until golden, then crush with a pestle in a small bowl. Add the white wine, mirin and yoghurt and stir to combine. Serve with the rolls.

GLUTEN-FREE

Mains

vegetarian LASAGNE

Serves 6–8

Preparation time: 25 minutes
Cooking time: 40 minutes

300 g (10½ oz) eggplant
 (aubergine), thinly sliced
300 g (10½ oz) sweet potato,
 peeled and thinly sliced
300 g (10½ oz) zucchini (courgettes),
 thinly sliced
200 g (7 oz) mushrooms, thinly sliced
2 tablespoons olive oil
Salt and pepper
375 g (13 oz) rice lasagne sheets
100 g (3½ oz) parmesan cheese, grated

Béchamel sauce
100 g (3½ oz) vegetable margarine,
 plus extra for greasing
100 g (3½ oz) rice flour
310 ml (10¾ fl oz/1¼ cups) soy milk

Preheat oven to 180°C (350°F/Gas 4).

Place the vegetables on a large baking tray, drizzle with the olive oil and season with a little salt and pepper. Bake for 25 minutes. Increase oven temperature to 200°C (400°F/Gas 6).

Meanwhile, to prepare the béchamel sauce, combine the margarine and rice flour in a saucepan over very low heat and cook for 2–3 minutes, stirring regularly, then increase the heat and add the soy milk gradually, whisking until thick.

Cook the lasagne sheets in boiling water for 2 minutes, then drain on paper towels.

Arrange the ingredients in a lightly greased rectangular baking dish in the following order: one layer of pasta, one layer of béchamel, one layer of roasted vegetables. Repeat once. Finish with a layer of pasta, the remaining béchamel sauce and the grated parmesan sprinkled on top.

Bake for 15 minutes or until golden.

Delicious with: A well-dressed mixed salad or seasonal raw vegetables.

NOGLU'S LASAGNE *bolognese*

Serves 6

Preparation time: 30 minutes
Cooking time: 45 minutes

2 tablespoons olive oil
500 g (1 lb 2 oz) minced (ground) beef
½ onion, chopped
2 garlic cloves, crushed
150 ml (5½ fl oz) tomato passata
  (puréed tomatoes)
1 teaspoon ground cumin
1 teaspoon ground coriander
1 teaspoon ground paprika
2 dried bay leaves
2 thyme sprigs
375 g (13 oz) rice lasagne sheets
150 g (5½ oz) parmesan cheese, grated

Béchamel sauce
100 g (3½ oz) vegetable margarine,
  plus extra for greasing
100 g (3½ oz) rice flour
310 ml (10¾ fl oz/1¼ cups) soy milk

Preheat oven to 200°C (400°F/Gas 6).

Heat 1 tablespoon of the olive oil in a frying pan, add the beef and brown for 1–2 minutes. Add the onion, garlic, tomato passata, spices and herbs. Cook gently for 20 minutes.

To prepare the béchamel sauce, combine the margarine and rice flour in a saucepan over very low heat and cook for 2–3 minutes, stirring regularly, then increase the heat and add the soy milk gradually, whisking until thick.

Cook the lasagne sheets in boiling water for 2 minutes, then drain on paper towels. Arrange the ingredients in a lightly greased rectangular baking dish in the following order: one layer of pasta, one layer of béchamel, one layer of meat sauce. Repeat the process once. Finish with a layer of pasta, the remaining béchamel sauce and the grated parmesan sprinkled on top.

Bake for 15 minutes or until golden.

Delicious with: A well-dressed mixed salad or seasonal raw vegetables.

penne WITH TOMATO AND ROCKET

Preparation time: 15 minutes
Cooking time: 10 minutes

250 g (9 oz) tinned organic reduced
  salt peeled tomatoes
2 tablespoons olive oil
1 pinch dried oregano
250 g (9 oz) rice penne
310 ml (10¾ fl oz/1¼ cups) organic
  chicken stock (or 1 organic
  stock/bouillon cube dissolved
  in 310 ml boiling water)
50 g (1¾ oz) sun-dried tomatoes
50 g (1¾ oz) rocket (arugula)
50 g (1¾ oz) parmesan cheese, shaved
Cherry tomatoes, to garnish (optional)

In a small saucepan, gently heat the tinned tomatoes with a tablespoon of the olive oil and the oregano for 6–7 minutes. Blend until smooth. Keep warm over very low heat.

Heat the remaining olive oil in another saucepan and sauté the penne for about 30 seconds, then ladle the stock over the pasta and cook for 3–4 minutes, or until *al dente*.

Pour into two large, deep plates, pour over the prepared tomato sauce and top with the sun-dried tomatoes, rocket and shaved parmesan.

Garnish with a few cherry tomatoes if you like and serve immediately.

MUSHROOM *risotto*

Serves 2

Preparation time: 20 minutes
Cooking time: 25 minutes

1 tablespoon olive oil
2 French shallots, finely chopped
100 g (3½ oz) mushrooms (mixed
    shiitake, morels, shimeji, or other
    mushroom of your choice), sliced
200 g (7 oz) rice (arborio or carnaroli)
60 ml (2 fl oz/¼ cup) dry white wine
500 ml (17 fl oz/2 cups) hot chicken stock
40 g (1½ oz) vegetable margarine
60 ml (2 fl oz/¼ cup) soy milk
50 g (1¾ oz) parmesan cheese, grated
About 30 g (1 oz/¾ cup) rocket (arugula)

Heat the olive oil in a frying pan and sweat the shallots for 4 minutes.

Add the mushrooms and brown for 2 minutes, then add the rice. When the rice becomes shiny and almost translucent, add the white wine. Reduce slightly, then add the stock as necessary, stirring constantly until the stock is absorbed.

Check that the rice is cooked — it should be *al dente* — then add the margarine and soy milk and stir for 1 minute.

Add the grated parmesan and rocket. Season to taste. Serve immediately.

BLACK RISOTTO WITH *squid*

Serves 2

Preparation time: 30 minutes
Cooking time: 35 minutes

1 tablespoon olive oil
2 French shallots, finely chopped
200 g (7 oz/1 cup) black rice, rinsed
60 ml (2 fl oz/¼ cup) dry white wine
500 ml (17 fl oz/2 cups) fish stock
   (1 organic stock/bouillon cube
   dissolved in 500 ml boiling water)
50 g (1¾ oz) cuttlefish ink
50 g (1¾ oz) vegetable margarine
20 g (¾ oz) preserved lemon, rind
   chopped into small pieces
100 g (3½ oz) squid, scored
½ teaspoon tamari (wheat-free
   soy sauce)
1 beetroot (beet)
3 baby carrots of different colours
Fresh herbs of choice, to garnish
   (coriander/cilantro, tarragon ...)

Heat the olive oil in a frying pan and sauté the shallots for 4–5 minutes, then add the black rice. Sauté for 5 minutes, then add the white wine and stir for 2 minutes to evaporate the alcohol. Add the fish stock and cuttlefish ink and cook gently for 20 minutes. Add the margarine and preserved lemon.

Heat the remaining olive oil in a separate frying pan and add the squid. Fry until just cooked, 1–2 minutes, then add the tamari to the pan.

Slice the vegetables very thinly (about 2 mm/¹⁄₁₆ inch), and drop them immediately into iced water.

Serve the rice in a deep plate topped with the squid and decorated with the vegetable slices and fresh herbs.

SAGE *gnocchi*

Serves 6

Preparation time: 20 minutes
Resting time: 3½ hours
Cooking time: 35 minutes

1 kg (2 lb 4 oz) potatoes
2 eggs, beaten
300 g (10½ oz) parmesan cheese, grated
20 g (¾ oz/1 cup) sage leaves
1½ tablespoons olive oil
200 g (7 oz) rice flour, plus
    extra for dusting
1 preserved lemon, rind finely diced
Finely grated zest of 1 lime
1 pinch salt
12 baby leeks
12 baby radishes
12 baby carrots

Peel the potatoes and cook them in boiling water for 20 minutes or until just cooked. Drain, pass them through a potato ricer or food mill, then allow them to cool for 30 minutes.

Add the eggs and parmesan to the cooled potato and mix together well.

Sauté the sage leaves in the olive oil in a frying pan for 4 minutes, setting a few fried sage leaves aside for the garnish, then purée in a small food processor.

Add the rice flour, sage purée, preserved lemon, lime zest and salt to the potato mixture and combine well again to form a potato dough.

Knead the dough by hand for 5 minutes, then divide into six pieces. Flour the pieces with rice flour and roll them into sausages 1 cm (½ inch) thick. Cut each roll into 3 cm (1¼ inch) pieces, flour them again, then make grooves in the gnocchi by rolling each one up and down a fork placed upside down on the work surface. Flour them again, place on a dry cloth and rest for 3 hours at room temperature.

Steam the baby vegetables for about 6 minutes or until just tender.

Bring a large saucepan of salted water to the boil and drop in the gnocchi. When they rise to the surface, let them cook for 3 minutes, then remove with a slotted spoon. Serve hot with the vegetables and reserved sage leaves.

BEEF AND *cheddar burger*

Preparation time: 15 minutes
Cooking time: 15 minutes

2 teaspoons olive oil
½ onion, thinly sliced
1 x 150 g (5½ oz) minced
   (ground) beef patty
1 slice cheddar cheese
1 gluten-free burger bun
1 tablespoon mayonnaise
5 baby spinach leaves
1 slice of tomato

Preheat oven to 200°C (400°F/Gas 6).

Heat 1 teaspoon of the olive oil in a frying pan over medium heat, add the onion and cook for 5 minutes or until caramelised.

Put the patty on a baking tray and place in the oven for 10 minutes or until cooked to your liking. Place the cheese on top for the final 5 minutes of cooking.

Meanwhile, cut the burger bun in half and brush the cut sides with the remaining olive oil. Brown in a separate frying pan.

Spread each of the toasted halves with mayonnaise. Place the base on a serving plate and top with the spinach, tomato, patty, onion and the top of the bun.

Delicious with: Boiled new potatoes browned in a frying pan with a little duck fat.

VEGETARIAN *tofu burger*

Preparation time: 20 minutes
Cooking time: 45 minutes

1 eggplant (aubergine), sliced
1 sweet potato, thinly sliced
3½ tablespoons olive oil, plus
   extra for brushing
Salt and pepper
2 onions, thinly sliced
200 g (7 oz) tofu
1 egg
2 tablespoons rice flour
2 tablespoons gluten-free breadcrumbs
2 gluten-free burger buns
60 g (2¼ oz) cheddar cheese,
   cut into 2 thin slices
100 g (3½ oz) mixed salad leaves

Preheat oven to 180°C (350°F/Gas 4).

Place the eggplant and sweet potato slices on a baking tray. Drizzle with 1 tablespoon of the olive oil, season with salt and pepper and roast for 20–25 minutes.

Sauté the onions in a frying pan with 1 tablespoon of the olive oil over low heat for about 10 minutes or until they are golden.

Cut the tofu into two equal portions. Combine the egg, rice flour and breadcrumbs in a large bowl, then dip the tofu in this mixture, coating each side well. Heat the remaining olive oil in a separate frying pan and fry the tofu until golden brown on all sides. Drain on paper towels.

Halve the burger buns. Brush a little olive oil on the cut sides and brown the oiled sides in a frying pan for about 1 minute until golden.

To assemble the burgers, lay two slices of eggplant on each base, then a piece of tofu, a slice of cheddar cheese and the onions. Top with the bun tops, hold the whole thing together with a wooden skewer and bake for 6–8 minutes to melt the cheddar. Serve with the roasted sweet potato and salad leaves.

ROASTED *vegetable* PIZZA

Serves 4

Preparation time: 30 minutes
Cooking time: 50 minutes

500 g (1 lb 2 oz) gluten-free
  bread dough (page 12)
100 g (3½ oz) mushrooms
100 g (3½ oz) zucchini (courgettes)
100 g (3½ oz) eggplant (aubergine)
100 g (3½ oz) capsicum (pepper)
½ onion
1 tablespoon olive oil, plus
  extra for drizzling
Rice flour, for dusting
50 g (1¾ oz/¼ cup) polenta
100 g (3½ oz/1⅔ cups) crumbled
  feta cheese
100 g (3½ oz) parmesan cheese,
  shaved
12 basil leaves

Tomato sauce

1 garlic clove, chopped
2 onions, chopped
2 tablespoons olive oil
440 g (15½ oz) tinned peeled tomatoes
1 teaspoon dried oregano
2½ tablespoons vergeoise blonde or
  light brown sugar (see note page 22)

Pesto

1 large bunch basil, leaves picked
1 garlic clove
50 g (1¾ oz) almonds or pine nuts
50 g (1¾ oz) parmesan cheese, grated
Juice of ½ lemon
60 ml (2 fl oz/¼ cup) olive oil

Preheat oven to 180°C (350°F/Gas 4).

Let the dough rise for 20 minutes.

For the tomato sauce, sauté the garlic and onion in the olive oil in a saucepan for 5 minutes over low heat, then add the tomatoes, oregano and sugar. Simmer for 20 minutes to reduce, stirring regularly. Season.

Place the pesto ingredients in a blender and process until smooth. Thin the pesto out with an extra tablespoon of olive oil if it is too thick. Adjust the seasoning with salt and pepper.

Wash the vegetables and cut them into slices about 5 mm (¼ inch) thick. Arrange them in a baking dish and pour over a little olive oil. Bake for 20–25 minutes. Increase the heat to 210°C (415°F/Gas 6–7).

Divide the bread dough into four equal pieces and knead them to form balls. Roll them out on a clean surface dusted with rice flour. With wet hands, stretch the dough out to make four circles of equal size.

Place a sheet of baking paper on a baking tray (prepare another if needed), scatter over the polenta and drizzle over a little olive oil before laying the pizza bases on top, without any topping. Cook the bases in the preheated oven for 15 minutes.

Remove the bases from the oven and add the toppings in the following order: tomato sauce, roasted vegetables, feta and shaved parmesan. Drizzle each pizza with 2 tablespoons of pesto and add a few leaves of fresh basil.

Return to the oven and bake for 6–8 minutes or until the vegetables are cooked and the cheese has melted.

californian PIZZA

Serves 4

Preparation time: 30 minutes
Cooking time: 50 minutes

500 g (1 lb 2 oz) gluten-free
   bread dough (page 12)
100 g (3½ oz) turkey breast,
   cut into cubes
2 tablespoons olive oil
Rice flour, for dusting
50 g (1¾ oz/¼ cup) polenta
2 avocados, peeled, stones removed
   and flesh thinly sliced
100 g (3½ oz) prosciutto
100 g (3½ oz) goat's cheese, crumbled
100 g (3½ oz/2¾ cups) rocket
   (arugula) (optional)
40 g (1½ oz/⅓ cup) grated
   parmesan cheese

Tomato sauce
1 garlic clove, chopped
2 onions, chopped
2 tablespoons olive oil
440 g (15½ oz) tinned peeled tomatoes
1 teaspoon dried oregano, plus
   extra for sprinkling
2½ tablespoons vergeoise blonde or
   light brown sugar (see note page 22)

Preheat oven to 210°C (415°F/Gas 6–7).

Let the dough rise for 20 minutes.

For the tomato sauce, sauté the garlic and onions in the olive oil in a saucepan for 5 minutes over low heat, then add the tomatoes, oregano and sugar. Simmer for 20 minutes to reduce, stirring regularly. Season.

Sauté the turkey breast cubes for a few minutes in a frying pan with 1 tablespoon of the olive oil.

Divide the bread dough into four equal pieces and knead them to form balls. Roll them out on a clean surface dusted with rice flour. With wet hands, stretch the dough out to make four circles of equal size.

Place a sheet of baking paper on a baking tray (prepare another if needed), scatter with polenta and drizzle over the remaining olive oil before laying the pizza bases on top. Cook in the oven for 15 minutes.

Remove the bases from the oven and add the toppings in the following order: tomato sauce, avocado, prosciutto and turkey. Scatter with the goat's cheese and rocket (if using), then top with parmesan.

Return to the oven and bake for 6–8 minutes or until the cheese has melted.

CLUB SANDWICH WITH *turkey* AND BLUE CHEESE

Serves 4

Preparation time: 15 minutes
Cooking time: 10 minutes

1 loaf of chickpea-buckwheat
   bread (page 154)
200 g (7 oz) sun-dried tomatoes
1½ tablespoons olive oil
2 avocados
Juice of 1 lemon
400 g (14 oz) cooked turkey
   breast, thinly sliced
200 g (7 oz) blue cheese,
   cut into four pieces
100 g (3½ oz/2¾ cups) rocket
   (arugula)

Preheat oven to 180°C (350°F/Gas 4).

Cut the bread into 12 thick slices and lightly toast them.

Place the sun-dried tomatoes and olive oil in a food processor and process to form a paste.

Peel the avocados, cut into slices and sprinkle with lemon juice to prevent them browning.

Spread one-quarter of the tomato paste on a slice of bread. Top with one-eighth of the turkey slices, then a slice of bread.

Place one-quarter of the avocado on top of this slice, then one-eighth of turkey, a piece of the blue cheese and rocket. Top with a slice of bread and secure with a skewer. Repeat to make four sandwiches. Place the sandwiches on a baking tray and bake for 8 minutes or until the cheese is melted.

Serve immediately.

Delicious with: A raw vegetable salad.

vegetarian CLUB SANDWICH

Serves 1
Preparation time: 15 minutes
Cooking time: 40 minutes

2 long slices of sweet potato,
    1 cm (½ inch) thick
2 slices of eggplant (aubergine), 1 cm
    (½ inch) thick
Olive oil
3 slices of gluten-free bread, sandwich-
    loaf shape (pages 152 and 154)
20 g (¾ oz) cheddar (or emmental)
    cheese, cut into 2 thin slices
1 tablespoon tapenade (recipe below)

Tapenade
100 g (3½ oz) pitted olives
50 g (1¾ oz) sun-dried tomatoes
1 onion, chopped
1 garlic clove, crushed
1 tablespoon olive oil
1 tablespoon lemon juice

Preheat oven to 200°C (400°F/Gas 6).

Place the sweet potato and eggplant slices on a baking tray. Drizzle with a little olive oil and bake for 25–30 minutes or until soft.

To prepare the tapenade, place all of the ingredients in a food processor and pulse to make a thick paste with a little texture.

Lightly toast the bread. Spread each slice of bread with the tapenade.

Top one slice of bread with half of the sweet potato, eggplant and cheese, then a slice of bread. Repeat.

Cut in half diagonally and secure each half with wooden skewers. Bake for 6–8 minutes to melt the cheese.

Delicious with: A salad of raw vegetables, dressed with lemon juice and olive oil.

soba noodles WITH CHICKEN BROTH

Serves 6

Preparation time: 20 minutes
Cooking time: 40 minutes

1 chicken stock (bouillon) cube
1 tablespoon tamari (wheat-
   free soy sauce)
1 tablespoon mirin (rice wine)
100 g (3½ oz) shiitake mushrooms
300 g (10½ oz) komatsuna
   (Japanese leafy vegetable) or
   spinach leaves if unavailable
6 eggs
600 g (1 lb 5 oz) soba noodles
   (pure buckwheat)
4 spring onions (scallions),
   thinly sliced
150 g (5½ oz) yam, grated

Make the broth by dissolving the chicken stock cube in 250 ml (9 fl oz/1 cup) of water. Reduce for 5 minutes, then add the tamari and mirin.

Cook the mushrooms in boiling salted water for 1 minute.

Steam the komatsuna or spinach for 10 minutes.

Soft-boil the eggs by gently immersing them in water heated to 63°C (145°F) for 30 minutes or cook them in barely simmering water for 3 minutes.

Cook the soba noodles in boiling salted water for 3 minutes. Drain the noodles, divide between six large bowls and pour over the hot broth. Top with the komatsuna or spinach and mushrooms, then the peeled soft-boiled eggs and the spring onions.

Serve with the grated yam in a small pot on the side.

tuna  TATAKI

Serves 2 as a main or 6 as a starter
Preparation time: 15 minutes
Resting time: 1 hour
Cooking time: 20 minutes

300 g (10½ oz) tuna fillet
500 ml (17 fl oz/2 cups) dashi vinegar
2 yellow capsicums (peppers),
    halved and deseeded
Olive oil
200 g (7 oz) fennel bulb
1 tablespoon sherry vinegar
1 avocado
2 teaspoons lemon juice
1 teaspoon ground coriander
3 spring onions (scallions), thinly sliced
1 preserved lemon, rind finely diced

Preheat oven to 180°C (350°F/Gas 4).

Slice the tuna fillet (or ask the fishmonger to do this) into triangular sections, each side about 4 cm (1½ inches). Heat a frying pan over medium heat and sear the tuna for a few seconds on each side. Place the tuna pieces in a bowl and immediately pour over the vinegar. Refrigerate for 1 hour.

Meanwhile, roast the yellow capsicums with a little olive oil for 20 minutes or until they start to brown. Cool for 1–2 minutes so they can be handled, then peel them and process the flesh with their juices.

Thinly slice the fennel and drop the slices immediately into iced water. Drain the slices and mix with the sherry vinegar and some salt and pepper.

Process the avocado flesh with the lemon juice and 1 tablespoon of olive oil. Season with the ground coriander and some salt and pepper.

Drain the tuna and slice into 5 mm (¼ inch) sections.

Spoon some of the capsicum purée across a plate. Arrange the slices of cold tuna on a plate, scatter over the spring onion and diced preserved lemon, and serve with the fennel and guacamole.

roasted cod WITH LEMON RICE

Serves 2

Preparation time: 20 minutes
Cooking time: 30 minutes

75 g (2½ oz/⅓ cup) rice
   (arborio or carnaroli)
2 witlofs (chicory/Belgian endives)
80 ml (2½ fl oz/⅓ cup) olive oil
Juice of 1 orange
1 teaspoon honey
300 g (10½ oz) cod fillets
1 preserved lemon, rind finely diced
2 coriander (cilantro) sprigs, chopped
2 teaspoons lemon juice
100 g (3½ oz) morels (sold
   cooked in jars)
2 spring onions (scallions),
   thinly sliced
Finely grated zest of 1 lemon

Preheat oven to 170°C (325°F/Gas 3).

Cook the rice according to the packet directions.

Cut the witlofs in half and sauté them in 2 tablespoons of olive oil in a frying pan. Salt lightly and when there is no more liquid, pour in the orange juice and honey and reduce for a further 5–6 minutes. Transfer to a blender and purée until smooth.

Place the cod on a baking tray, drizzle with the remaining olive oil and season. Bake for 10 minutes. Check the cod by inserting the tip of a knife into the thickest part and remove from the oven when it is just cooked.

Combine the preserved lemon, chopped coriander and lemon juice.

Spoon the puréed witlof mixture onto two plates and gently spread out with the back of a spoon. Divide the rice between the plates, place the cod on top and garnish with the spring onion, preserved lemon mix and morels. Sprinkle over the lemon zest and serve.

crumbed veal AND ROOT VEGETABLE GRATIN

Serves 2

Preparation time: 15 minutes
Cooking time: 1 hour

1 red capsicum (pepper)
200 g (7 oz) root vegetables
   (e.g. beetroot/beets of
   different colours, turnips)
3–4 tablespoons béchamel
   sauce (recipe below)
50 g (1¾ oz) hard sheep's
   milk cheese, grated
300 g (10½ oz) veal topside
1 egg, beaten
Gluten-free breadcrumbs
Olive oil

Béchamel sauce
50 g (1¾ oz) vegetable margarine
1½ tablespoons rice flour
150 ml (5 fl oz) soy milk

Preheat oven to 180°C (350°F/Gas 4).

Halve and deseed the capsicum, place on a baking tray and bake for 30 minutes. Peel and purée in a food processor until smooth — add a little water if necessary to achieve a pouring consistency. Season.

Bring a medium saucepan of water to the boil and add the unpeeled root vegetables. Boil for 10 minutes or until just tender. Drain, peel and cut into small cubes. Place in a small 250 ml (9 fl oz/1 cup) baking dish.

Preheat grill (broiler).

Meanwhile, to prepare the béchamel sauce, combine the margarine and flour in a small saucepan. Cook for 2–3 minutes over very low heat, stirring, then increase the heat and add the soy milk while whisking until thickened. Spoon enough béchamel over the prepared vegetables to cover.

Top with the cheese and place under the grill for 10 minutes or until golden.

Cut the veal into two pieces, dip in the egg, then the breadcrumbs to coat. Season.

Heat 1 cm (½ inch) of olive oil in a frying pan over medium–high heat and fry the veal for 3–4 minutes on each side until crisp and golden.

Serve with the capsicum sauce and vegetable gratin.

macaroni AND HAM GRATIN

Serves 2 as a main or 6 as a starter
Preparation time: 20 minutes
Cooking time: 30 minutes

300 g (10½ oz) gluten-free macaroni
30 g (1 oz) ham, cut into small pieces
50 g (1¾ oz) onion, sliced
2 tablespoons olive oil
50 g (1¾ oz) grated Comté or
  gruyere cheese

Béchamel sauce
100 g (3½ oz) vegetable margarine
100 g (3½ oz) rice flour
310 ml (10¾ fl oz/1¼ cups) soy milk

Cook the pasta in boiling salted water with 1 tablespoon
of the olive oil for 3 minutes, or according to the packet
directions, then drain.

For the béchamel sauce, combine the margarine and
rice flour in a small saucepan, cook for 2–3 minutes over
very low heat, stirring regularly, then increase the heat
and add the soy milk gradually, whisking until thickened.

Sauté the ham and onions in a frying pan in the
remaining olive oil for 5 minutes.

Preheat grill (broiler).

Add the drained pasta and béchamel sauce to the frying
pan and adjust the seasoning with salt and pepper. Pour
into a baking dish, sprinkle with the cheese and place
under the grill for 5–6 minutes to brown the top well.

Serve with a few slices of toast.

veal blanquette WITH BLACK RICE

Serves 6

Preparation time: 30 minutes
Cooking time: 3 hours

1 kg (2 lb 4 oz) veal breast, cut into pieces
2 onions, cut into large pieces
2 carrots, cut into large pieces
1 leek, pale part only, cut
   into large pieces
300 g (10½ oz/1½ cups) black rice
50 g (1¾ oz) vegetable margarine
50 g (1¾ oz/¼ cup) rice flour
100 ml (3½ fl oz) soy milk
1 teaspoon ground cumin
1 teaspoon curry powder
1 teaspoon ground coriander
Chives, chopped, to garnish

In a large saucepan bring enough water to just cover the veal to a boil. Add the pieces of veal and once the water returns to the boil, skim away any foam from the surface and add the vegetables. Reduce the heat and simmer gently for 2 hours.

Remove the vegetables with a slotted spoon and keep them warm. Remove the meat and set aside. Reduce the cooking liquid by half by simmering it gently for 20–30 minutes.

Meanwhile, cook the rice according to the packet directions.

Melt the margarine in a medium saucepan and add the rice flour. Cook very gently for 5 minutes, stirring regularly. Increase the heat and add the reduced cooking liquid to the roux, in several stages, stirring constantly. Add the soy milk and spices. Adjust the seasoning.

Place a portion of rice and vegetables in six deep plates with the meat. Pour over the sauce and garnish with the chives.

GLUTEN-FREE

Desserts

brownies

Serves 8–10

Preparation time: 15 minutes
Cooking time: 30 minutes

180 g (6 oz) dark chocolate
   (at least 60% cocoa)
160 g (5½ oz) butter (or
   vegetable margarine)
4 eggs
280 g (10 oz/1¼ cups) sugar
150 g (5½ oz) gluten-free
   flour mix (page 13)
100 g (3½ oz/1 cup) pecans,
   chopped

Preheat oven to 180°C (350°F/Gas 4).

In a medium saucepan, gently melt the chocolate and butter together and mix well. Allow to cool.

Whisk the eggs and sugar together, then add them to the melted chocolate mixture, whisking to combine.

Add the flour mix while continuing to whisk to avoid lumps. Pour the mixture into a round 20 cm (8 inch) cake tin. Scatter the chopped pecans on top and bake for 25–30 minutes or until the brownie has set but the centre is still a little soft and melting.

vegan CHOCOLATE CAKE

Serves 8–10

Preparation time: 15 minutes
Cooking time: 30 minutes

420 g (15 oz) gluten-free
   flour mix (page 13)
380 g (13½ oz) sugar
80 g (2¾ oz/¾ cup) cocoa powder
3 teaspoons bicarbonate of
   soda (baking soda)
2 teaspoons salt
1 vanilla bean, halved lengthways
   and seeds scraped
500 ml (17 fl oz/2 cups) cold water
150 ml (5 fl oz) coconut oil,
   plus extra for greasing
1½ tablespoons cider vinegar
50 g (1¾ oz/⅓ cup) hazelnuts

Coffee cream
220 g (7¾ oz) vegetable margarine
400 g (14 oz) icing (confectioners')
   sugar
1 teaspoon coffee extract

Preheat oven to 180°C (350°F/Gas 4).

Combine the flour mix, sugar, cocoa, bicarbonate of soda, salt and vanilla seeds. Add the water, coconut oil and vinegar. Mix well until you have a smooth batter.

Grease two round 24 cm (9½ inch) cake tins, then pour the batter into the tins and smooth the tops with a spatula.

Bake the cakes for 30 minutes or until a skewer inserted into the middle comes out clean. Cool in the tins.

Make the coffee cream by beating the margarine and icing sugar together until light and airy. Add the coffee extract and mix again. Keep this cream in the fridge until you assemble the cake.

Toast the hazelnuts in a dry frying pan, making sure not to burn them.

When the cakes are cool, spread with the coffee cream and gently place one on top of the other. Scatter over the roughly chopped toasted hazelnuts.

Delicious with: Fresh strawberries.

chocolate FONDANT CAKE

Serves 5

Preparation time: 15 minutes
Cooking time: 10 minutes

100 g (3½ oz) dark chocolate
　　(at least 60% cocoa)
90 g (3¼ oz) butter (or vegetable
　　margarine)
3 eggs
100 g (3½ oz) sugar
45 g (1½ oz/¼ cup) rice flour
1 tablespoon tapioca starch

Preheat oven to 180°C (350°F/Gas 4).

Gently melt the chocolate and butter together in a saucepan and combine. Allow to cool.

Whisk the eggs with the sugar and add to the melted chocolate mixture, mixing well.

Combine the rice flour and starch, add to the chocolate mixture and stir until just combined.

Divide the batter into five round 8 cm (3¼ inch) baking dishes. Bake for 8 minutes. Serve warm.

Delicious with: Fresh fruit or sorbet.

PINEAPPLE-MANGO *crumble*

Serves 10

Preparation time: 15 minutes
Cooking time: 25 minutes

Crumble mixture
100 g (3½ oz) rice flour
100 g (3½ oz) raw (demerara) sugar
100 g (3½ oz/1 cup) almond meal
90 g (3¼ oz) cold butter (or vegetable margarine), cut into cubes
60 g (2 oz/¼ cup) flaked almonds

Fruit mixture
1 small pineapple
3 mangoes
1½ tablespoons sugar
½ vanilla bean, halved lengthways and seeds scraped
1 pinch ground cardamom

Preheat oven to 180°C (350°F/Gas 4).

Combine the rice flour, sugar and almond meal in a large bowl, then add the cold butter.

Using your fingertips, work the butter into the flour mixture until it resembles coarse breadcrumbs, then add the flaked almonds, mixing together gently. Keep this mixture in the refrigerator while preparing the fruit.

Peel the pineapple and mangoes and cut them into small cubes.

Combine the sugar, vanilla seeds and cardamom in a clean bowl and add the fruit. Mix well and divide into 10 individual moulds (e.g. crème brûlée ramekins). Sprinkle 30–35 g (1–1¼ oz) of the crumble mixture on top of each one and bake for 25 minutes or until the crumble is golden and crunchy. Serve hot.

pear-chocolate TARTLETS

Makes 8 small tarts

Preparation time: 20 minutes
Cooking time: 50 minutes

4 pears
1 quantity sweet pastry (page 14)
150 g (5½ oz) flaked almonds
Rice flour, for dusting

Almond–chocolate cream
150 g (5½ oz) dark chocolate
    (at least 60% cocoa)
100 g (3½ oz) sugar
150 g (5½ oz) vegetable margarine (or
    soft butter), plus extra for greasing
3 eggs
100 g (3½ oz/1 cup) almond meal

Syrup
275 g (9¾ oz/1¼ cups) sugar
1 vanilla bean, halved lengthways
    and seeds scraped
1 litre (35 fl oz/4 cups) water

Preheat oven to 180°C (350°F/Gas 4).

To prepare the syrup, put the sugar, vanilla bean and seeds in a saucepan with the water and bring to the boil, stirring to dissolve the sugar. Add the peeled pears, cover the surface with baking paper and cook over low heat for 30 minutes. Once the pears are cooked, carefully remove them from the poaching liquid with a slotted spoon and leave to cool on paper towels.

For the cream, gently melt the chocolate. Mix the sugar and margarine in a large bowl and add the eggs one at a time, mixing well after each, then add the almond meal and melted chocolate.

Grease eight individual loose-based tart (flan) tins or 8 cm (3¼ inch) pastry rings.

Dust a clean surface with rice flour, roll out the pastry and cut out eight rounds the size of the individual tins that will be used for the tarts. Line the tins with the pastry.

Cut each poached pear in half, remove the seeds and core, then cut into thin slices.

Half-fill each tart shell with chocolate cream and arrange the slices of pear on top. Sprinkle the flaked almonds around the pear.

Bake for 20 minutes or until the cream is firm to the touch.

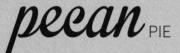

pecan PIE

Serves 8

Preparation time: 20 minutes
Cooking time: 25 minutes

1 quantity sweet pastry (page 14)
150 g (5½ oz) vergeoise blonde or light
  brown sugar (see note page 22)
150 g (5½ oz) soft butter
  (or vegetable margarine)
1 egg
60 g (2¼ oz/½ cup) chopped pecans
250 g (9 oz/2½ cups) whole pecans

Preheat oven to 180°C (350°F/Gas 4).

Line a 24 cm (9½ inch) tart (flan) tin with pastry and blind bake for 10 minutes (see tip on page 14).

Beat the sugar and butter together, then add the egg and chopped pecans. Mix to combine. Pour this mixture over the precooked pastry base, then decorate with the whole pecans.

Bake for 15 minutes or until the pie has formed a crust that's firm to the touch. Allow it to cool before removing from the tin.

Delicious with: A scoop of vanilla ice cream.

cheesecake

Makes 8–10 portions

Preparation time: 25 minutes
Cooking time: 1 hour, 10 minutes
Resting time: 24 hours

Rice flour, for dusting
1 quantity sweet pastry (page 14)
450 g (1 lb) cream cheese, at
    room temperature
450 g (1 lb) smooth fromage blanc
    (20% fat) or ricotta cheese
250 g (9 oz) sugar
½ vanilla bean, halved lengthways
    and seeds scraped
30 g (1 oz/¼ cup) cornflour
    (cornstarch)
4 eggs
Raspberry (or strawberry) jam

Preheat oven to 180°C (350°F/Gas 4).

Dust a clean surface with rice flour and roll out the pastry until 5 mm (¼ inch) thick. Place in a greased 26 cm (10½ inch) spring-form cake tin. Bake this base for 15–20 minutes or until it colours slightly.

Beat the cream cheese on a low speed until smooth, then add the fromage blanc or ricotta, a little at a time to avoid lumps. When the mix is smooth, add the sugar and the vanilla seeds, then the cornflour. Add the eggs one at a time and continue to mix on a low speed for 2 minutes until combined.

Pour the cheese mixture onto the base. Place a few teaspoonfuls of jam on top of the filling and make a pretty design using a skewer. Bake for about 45–50 minutes.

The cheesecake can still be a bit soft in the middle, but it should be quite firm around the edge. Turn off the oven and leave the cheesecake in the oven for another 10 minutes. Remove and let it cool at room temperature. Once it is completely cool, cover with plastic wrap and place in the refrigerator overnight.

Enjoy the next day with fresh berries.

pineapple UPSIDE-DOWN CAKE

Serves 8

Preparation time: 20 minutes
Cooking time: 30 minutes

1 small pineapple
185 g (6½ oz) gluten-free flour mix (page 13)
1 teaspoon baking powder
100 g (3½ oz) sugar
½ vanilla bean, halved lengthways
    and seeds scraped
1 teaspoon ground cardamom
2 eggs
80 ml (2½ fl oz/⅓ cup) canola oil
200 ml (7 fl oz) soy milk (or rice milk)

Caramel
150 g (5½ oz) vergeoise sugar
    (see note page 22)
75 g (2½ oz) butter (or vegetable
    margarine), plus extra for greasing

Preheat oven to 180°C (350°F/Gas 4).

Peel and core the pineapple and cut into slices. Cut these slices into pieces and arrange in a greased 24 cm (9½ inch) spring-form cake tin.

Make the caramel by combining the sugar and butter in a small saucepan and cooking over medium heat until bubbles appear. Once the mixture is well coloured, remove from the heat and pour evenly over the pineapple.

Combine the flour mix, baking powder, sugar, vanilla seeds and cardamom in a large bowl.

In another bowl, combine the eggs, canola oil and milk. Combine the two mixtures and mix together well. Pour the prepared batter over the pineapple in the cake tin. Use a spatula if necessary to spread out the batter so it completely covers the pineapple. Bake for 25–30 minutes or until a skewer inserted into the middle comes out clean.

Allow the cake to cool for 15–20 minutes before placing a plate over the top and inverting it onto the plate (be careful as there may be hot caramel).

polenta AND ORANGE CAKE

Serves 8

Preparation time: 15 minutes
Cooking time: 55 minutes

210 g (7½ oz) butter, plus
  extra for greasing
225 g (8 oz) sugar
3 eggs
225 g (8 oz/2¼ cups) almond meal
100 g (3½ oz) polenta
1½ tablespoons rice flour
25 g (1 oz) tapioca starch
½ teaspoon baking powder
Finely grated zest of 2 oranges
Juice of 1 orange

Preheat oven to 160°C (315°F/Gas 2–3).

Beat the butter and sugar in the bowl of a mixer until light and airy, then gently add the eggs, one at a time, beating after each.

Add the almond meal, polenta, flour, starch and baking powder, then the zest of the oranges. Mix to combine.

Pour the mixture into a greased loaf (bar) tin, or eight 8 cm (3¼ inch) tart (flan) tins if you like — the cooking time will be considerably less. Bake for 50–55 minutes or until a skewer inserted into the middle comes out clean.

When the cake comes out of the oven, drizzle with the juice of one of the oranges. Serve warm or cold.

Delicious with: Baked plums or a rhubarb compote and whipped cream.

pistachio-berry TARTLETS

Makes 8 small tarts

Preparation time: 20 minutes
Cooking time: 20 minutes

Rice flour, for dusting
1 quantity sweet pastry (page 14)
Raspberry jam
250 g (9 oz/2 cups) raspberries
250 g (9 oz/1⅔ cups) strawberries
100 g (3½ oz/⅔ cup) blueberries
100 g (3½ oz/¾ cup) blackberries
100 g (3½ oz) redcurrants

Pistachio cream

100 g (3½ oz) sugar
110 g (3¾ oz) vegetable
   margarine (or butter)
30 g (1 oz/¼ cup) cornflour (cornstarch)
2 eggs
35 g (1¼ oz/¼ cup) ground pistachios
100 g (3½ oz/1 cup) almond meal

Preheat oven to 180°C (350°F/Gas 4).

To prepare the pistachio cream, mix the sugar, margarine and cornflour together well. Add the eggs one at a time, then the ground pistachios and almond meal.

Dust a clean surface with rice flour, roll out the pastry and cut out rounds to fit eight 8–10 cm (3½–4 inch) tart (flan) tins. Line the tins with the pastry. Half-fill each tart shell with the pistachio cream and bake in the oven for 20 minutes or until the cream is firm to the touch.

Brush over a thin layer of raspberry jam. Cool and remove from tins. Decorate by carefully placing the berries on top.

matcha  TEA CAKE

Serves 8

Preparation time: 10 minutes
Cooking time: 45 minutes

190 g (6¼ oz) gluten-free
   flour mix (page 13)
150 g (5½ oz) sugar
1 teaspoon xanthan gum
1 teaspoon baking powder
1 teaspoon matcha tea powder
2 eggs
80 ml (2½ fl oz/⅓ cup) canola
   oil, plus extra for greasing
200 ml (7 fl oz) soy milk or rice milk
½ vanilla bean, halved lengthways
   and seeds scraped
Icing (confectioners') sugar, for dusting

Preheat oven to 180°C (350°F/Gas 4).

Combine the flour mix, sugar, xanthan gum, baking powder and matcha tea powder in a large bowl.

Whisk the eggs, canola oil and milk together in another bowl. Add the wet mixture to the dry ingredients, stir in the vanilla seeds and mix. Pour the batter into a greased 1.25–1.5 litre (44–52 fl oz/5–6 cup) loaf (bar) tin and bake for 40–45 minutes.

Cool in the tin, dust with icing sugar, then serve the cake with fresh berries.

Variation: Gently fold in 100 g (3½ oz) raspberries and/or strawberries and/or ripe redcurrants just before pouring the batter into the tin.

GLUTEN-FREE

Breads

chestnut FLOUR BREAD

Serves 8–10

Preparation time: 15 minutes
Resting time: 30 minutes
Cooking time: 35 minutes

435 ml (15¼ fl oz/1¾ cups) water
1 tablespoon olive oil, plus
    extra for greasing
1 teaspoon cider vinegar
3 eggs
100 g (3½ oz) chickpea flour (besan)
100 g (3½ oz) rice flour
50 g (1¾ oz) chestnut flour
125 g (4½ oz/1 cup) tapioca starch
125 g (4½ oz/⅔ cup) potato starch
2 teaspoons salt
1 tablespoon sugar
3¼ teaspoons xanthan gum
1 tablepsoon dried yeast
50 g (1¾ oz) walnuts, very finely chopped
50 g (1¾ oz) pecans, very finely chopped

Preheat oven to 180°C (350°F/Gas 4).

Mix the water, oil, vinegar and eggs in the bowl of a mixer.

In another bowl, combine the flours, starches, salt, sugar and xanthan gum, then add the yeast.

Add the dry ingredients to the wet and mix for 2 minutes on a low speed. Add the walnuts and pecans and mix through.

Pour the dough into a greased loaf (bar) tin. Smooth the surface of the dough with wet hands. Cover with a dry cloth and let stand for 30 minutes at room temperature.

Bake for 30–35 minutes. If you have a probe cooking thermometer, check the temperature inside the loaf; it should be 90°C (194°F) when it comes out of the oven. Turn the bread out immediately to prevent moisture condensing in the tin.

Delicious with: A savoury meal and/or cheese.

chickpea-buckwheat BREAD

Serves 6–8

Preparation time: 15 minutes
Resting time: 30 minutes
Cooking time: 35 minutes

435 ml (15¼ fl oz/1¾ cups) water
1 tablespoon olive oil
1 teaspoon cider vinegar
3 eggs
125 g (4½ oz) chickpea flour (besan)
50 g (1¾ oz) buckwheat flour
100 g (3½ oz) rice flour
125 g (4½ oz/1 cup) tapioca starch
125 g (4½ oz/⅔ cup) potato starch
2 teaspoons salt
1 tablespoon sugar
3¼ teaspoons xanthan gum
1 tablepsoon dried yeast

Preheat oven to 180°C (350°F/Gas 4).

Mix together the water, oil, vinegar and eggs in a mixer.

In another bowl, combine the flours, starches, salt, sugar and xanthan gum, then add the yeast.

Add the dry ingredients to the wet and mix for 2 minutes on a low speed.

Pour the dough into a greased loaf (bar) tin. Smooth the surface of the dough with wet hands. Cover with a dry cloth and let stand for 30 minutes at room temperature.

Bake for 30–35 minutes. If you have a probe cooking thermometer, check the temperature inside the loaf; it should be 90°C (194°F) when it comes out of the oven. Turn the bread out immediately to prevent moisture condensing in the tin.

This recipe is similar to the gluten-free bread dough on page 12 but we've added buckwheat for a lovely brown colour and a stronger nutty flavour.

Delicious with: Salads and other savoury dishes, or have it for breakfast.

muesli BREAD

Serves 8–10

Preparation time: 15 minutes
Cooking time: 35 minutes

50 g (1¾ oz) raisins or diced cranberries
50 g (1¾ oz) dried apricots,
   coarsely chopped
1 quantity gluten-free bread dough
   (page 12), prepared to mixing stage
50 g (1¾ oz) almonds
50 g (1¾ oz) hazelnuts or pecans
Oil, for greasing

Preheat oven to 180°C (350°F/Gas 4).

Soak the dried fruit in warm water for 15 minutes then drain and add to the bread dough during the last minute of mixing, along with the almonds and hazelnuts.

Tip the dough into a greased loaf (bar) tin. Smooth the surface of the dough with wet hands. Cover with a dry cloth and let stand for 30 minutes at room temperature.

Bake for 30–35 minutes. If you have a probe cooking thermometer, check the temperature inside the loaf; it should be 90°C (194°F) when it comes out of the oven. Turn the bread out immediately to prevent moisture condensing in the tin.

Delicious with: Cheese, or freshly baked for breakfast.

RECIPE INDEX

Acknowledgements

Thanks from the bottom of my heart to everyone who believed in NOGLU, who encouraged me and helped me make it real: David Lanher, without whom the project would have remained in the dream stage, Olivia Deslandes, Frédérick Grasser-Hermé, Nadia Sammut, Pierre Hermé, Renaud Marcille, Nicolas Gauduin, Mike Pearson, Steve from À la Mère de Famille.
Thanks also to Carmine Luongo, Giusepe Manzaro, Gianni Frasi, Reynald Bronzoni and Florence Lallement.

Paris suppliers

Up Store, Merci, Conran Shop, Caravane
www.miaow-design.fr

Noglu – Gluten-free Restaurant and Food Store

16 passage des Panoramas – 75002 Paris
contact@noglu.fr – tel. 01 40 26 41 24

Our recommended sites

www.exquidia.com
www.naturgie.com
www.chocolatdardenne.com
www.nouveauxrobinson.fr
www.bio-c-bon.com
+ all sites specialising in gluten-free and allergen-free products.

First published by Marabout in 2013.
Published in 2014 by Murdoch Books, an imprint of Allen & Unwin.

Murdoch Books Australia
83 Alexander Street
Crows Nest NSW 2065
Phone: +61 (0) 2 8425 0100
Fax: +61 (0) 2 9906 2218
www.murdochbooks.com.au
info@murdochbooks.com.au

Murdoch Books UK
Erico House, 6th Floor
93–99 Upper Richmond Road
Putney, London SW15 2TG
Phone: +44 (0) 20 8785 5995
Fax: +44 (0) 20 8785 5985
www.murdochbooks.co.uk
info@murdochbooks.co.uk

For corporate orders & custom publishing contact
Noel Hammond, National Business Development Manager, Murdoch Books Australia

Publisher: Corinne Roberts
Photographer: Akiko Ida
Stylist: Sabrina Fauda-Rôle
Translator: Melissa McMahon
Editor: Sophia Oravecz
Food editor: Grace Campbell
Editorial manager: Katie Bosher
Production: Mary Bjelobrk

A cataloguing-in-publication entry is available from the catalogue of the National Library of Australia at www.nla.gov.au.
A catalogue record for this book is available from the British Library.

Colour reproduction by Splitting Image, Clayton, Victoria.
Printed by 1010 Printing.

IMPORTANT: Those who might be at risk from the effects of salmonella poisoning (the elderly, pregnant women, young children and those suffering from immune deficiency diseases) should consult their doctor with any concerns about eating raw eggs.

OVEN GUIDE: You may find cooking times vary depending on the oven you are using. For fan-forced ovens, as a general rule, set the oven temperature to 20°C (35°F) lower than indicated in the recipe.

MEASURES GUIDE: We have used 20 ml (4 teaspoon) tablespoon measures. If you are using a 15 ml (3 teaspoon) tablespoon add an extra teaspoon of the ingredient for each tablespoon specified.